AAN6153

D0368778

Poems for a New Mother

MOMENTS TO CHERISH

WATERCOLORS BY
GAIL ROTH

IDEALS PUBLICATIONS
NASHVILLE, TENNESSEE

ISBN 0-8249-5845-4

Published by Ideals Publications, a division of Guideposts
535 Metroplex Drive, Suite 250, Nashville, Tennessee 37211
www.idealsbooks.com

Color separations by Precision Color Graphics, Franklin, Wisconsin
Printed and bound in the U.S.A. by Inland Press/Inland Book

Library of Congress Cataloging-in-Publications Data is on file.

10 9 8 7 6 5 4 3 2 1

POEMS SELECTED BY PEGGY SCHAEFER
DESIGNED BY EVE DEGRIE

ACKNOWLEDGMENTS

FLANNERY, MAUREEN TOLMAN. "Bond" from *Mothers and Daughters*. Copyright © 2001 by June Cotner, published by Harmony
Books. Used by permission of the author. GIBRAN, KAHLIL. "On Children" from *The Prophet*. Copyright © 1923 by Kahlil
Gibran and renewed 1951 by Administrators C.T.A. of the Kahlil Gibran Estate and Mary G. Gibran. Used by permission of
Alfred A. Knopf, a division of Random House, Inc. and the Gibran National Committee. MACGREGOR, JILL NOBLIT. "Concep-
tion" from *Mothers and Daughters*. Copyright © 2001 by June Cotner, published by Harmony Books. Used by permission of the
author. PASTAN, LINDA. "Duet for One Voice" from *A Fraction of Darkness, Poems by Linda Pastan*. Copyright © 1985 by Linda
Pastan. Published by W.W. Norton and Company. PEARSON, CAROL LYNN. "Needed" from *Day-Old Child and Other Celebrations
of Motherhood* by Carol Lynn Pearson. Published by Gibbs Smith, Salt Lake City, 2001. Used with permission. POTOS, ANDREA.
"With Child" from *Mothers and Daughters*. Copyright © 2001 by June Cotner, published by Harmony Books. Used by permis-
sion of the author. WINTERS, ANNE. "The Chair by the Window" and "Night Light" from *The Key to the City*. Copyright © 1986
by the Chicago University Press. Reprinted by permission of the author. WRIGHT, NANCY MEANS. "Collage: Mother, Daughter,
Child, and Book" from *Claiming the Spirit Within* Compiled by Marilyn Sewell, published by Beacon Press, Boston. Copyright ©
1996. Our sincere thanks to the following authors whom we were unable to locate: Ellen Bass for "There are times in life when
one does the right thing"; Mona K. Guldswog for "Baby's Here...Congratulations"; Margaret H. Hasbargen for "Journey";
Maureen Hawkins for "The Miracle"; Kim Nam Jo for "My Baby Has No Name Yet", translated by Ko Wan in *Contemporary
Korean Poetry*, published by University of Iowa Press, 1970. Evangeline Paterson for "A Wish for My Children."

All possible care has been taken to fully acknowledge the ownership and use of every selection in this book. If any mistakes or
omissions have occurred, they will be corrected in subsequent editions, provided notification is sent to the publisher.

CONTENTS

A MOTHER
IS . . .

THE CREATION OF MOTHERS

When God thought of mother,
He must have laughed with satisfaction
and framed it quickly—
so rich, so deep, so divine,
so full of soul, power, and beauty
was the conception.

—HENRY WARD BEECHER

What Is a Mother?

God thought to give the sweetest thing
In His almighty power
To earth; and deeply pondering
What it should be — one hour
In fondest joy and love of heart
Outweighing every other —
He moved the gates of heaven apart
And gave to earth a mother!

— G. Newell Lovejoy

MOTHERHOOD

Womanliness means only motherhood;
All love begins and ends there—roams enough,
But, having run the circle, rests at home.

—ROBERT BROWNING

MOTHERS

I think God took the fragrance of a flower,
A pure white flower which blooms not for world praise
But which makes sweet and beautiful some bower;
The compassion of the dew, which gently lays
Reviving freshness on the fainting earth
And gives to all the tired things new birth;

The steadfastness and radiance of stars
Which lift the soul above the confining bar;
The gladness of fair dawns; the sunset's peace;
Contentment which from "trivial rounds" asks
    no release;
The life which finds its greatest joy in deeds of love
    for others—
I think God took these precious things and made of
    them the mothers.

—AUTHOR UNKNOWN

MOTHER-LOVE

The love of a mother is never exhausted.
It never changes; it never tires;
It endures through all; in good repute, in bad repute,
In the face of the world's condemnation,
A mother's love still lives on.

—WASHINGTON IRVING

No Lovelier Pair

Mother and the baby! Oh, I know no
    lovelier pair,
For all the dreams of all the world are
    hovering round them there.
And be the baby in the cot or nestling in
    her arms,
    The picture they present is one with
    never-fading charm.

    Mother and the baby—and the mother's
    eyes aglow
With joys that only mothers see and only
    mothers know!

And here is all there is to strife and all there
    is to fame
And all that men have struggled for since
    first a baby came.

I never see this lovely pair nor hear the
    mother sing
The lullabies of babyhood, but I start
    wondering
How much of everyone today the world
    thinks wise or brave
Is of the songs the mother sang and of the
    strength she gave.

—EDGAR A. GUEST

THE ESSENCE OF MOTHER

Mother is food;
She is love;
She is warmth;
She is earth.
To be loved by her
Means to be alive,
To be rooted,
To be at home.
—ERICH FROMM

DEAR MOTHER

O God, since ever I could speak,
My voice has fallen on faithful ears,
'Twas "Mother" in my triumph hour,
And "Mother" in my time of tears.
— LAURA C. REDDEN

MY MOTHER

Who fed me from her gentle breast
And hushed me in her arms to rest
And on my cheek sweet kisses pressed?
    My mother.

When sleep forsook my open eye,
Who was it sung sweet lullaby
And rocked me that I should not cry?
    My mother.

Who sat and watched my infant head
When sleeping in my cradle bed
And tears of sweet affection shed?
    My mother.

Who taught my infant lips to pray,
To love God's holy word and day,
And walk in wisdom's pleasant way?
    My mother.

When thou art feeble, old and gray,
My healthy arm shall be thy stay,
And I will soothe thy pains away,
    My mother.

And when I see thee hang thy head,
'Twill be my turn to watch thy bed
And tears of sweet affection shed,
    My mother.

—JANE TAYLOR

AWAITING
BABY'S
ARRIVAL

With Child

My life as I always claimed it
is already receding
further and further from me each moment—
just as the stars reached beyond
their original birth
toward the far edges of the universe,
an unstoppable expansion
that is my old life leaving
as the new moves in
to take its place at the center.

—Andrea Potos

THE CONCEPTION

Suddenly, you are. In an instant,
A fraction of a nanosecond;
Somewhere between was not and is,
The not yet and now—you become.

Unaware of your presence; yet you are there.
Silently, without detection,
You come into being and take your place.

You change me, rearrange me, without request.
You mold me into what you need;
My entire being complies.

A part of me, yet your own.
Miraculous metamorphosis within my womb;
That chrysalis of life.

Lost in wonder.
Both blessing and burden are mine, as a piece of eternity
Lodges deep within my members.

Part of an eternal plan set in motion.
And I, the chosen vessel, stand in awe;
blessed,
humbled,
undone.

—JILL NOBLIT MACGREGOR

NEEDED

The earth needs only nature.
If spring follows snow,
If new seeds swell,
Earth will go on and on,
Content.

I have watched with folded hands—
An uneasy guest.

But now suddenly I am nature.
And I am needed
As all tomorrow's orchards
Need the present tree.

How good—
This nine-month indispensability.
—CAROL LYNN PEARSON

THE MIRACLE

Before you were conceived
    I wanted you;
Before you were born
    I loved you;
Before you were here an hour,
    I would die for you.
This is the miracle of life.
The pain, so great,
was more than the throbbing of your final journey
into my love
But part of a process
that came accompanied with

New Life,
New Consciousness,
New Understanding,
New Wisdom,
A bigger heart
To accommodate
New Love.
At last Liberation,
At last Freedom.
How special, how valuable,
How close to all things right.

Nine months of worry and expectation
Brought more than imagination can conjure.
Never really knew
Until . . .
I feel you coming,
I am ready for you,
I am ready for life,
I am rejuvenated.
I am Blessed
with the gift of life.
— MAUREEN HAWKINS

To My Unborn Son

"My son!" What simple, beautiful words!
    "My boy!" What a wonderful phrase!
We're counting the months till you come to us—
    The months and the weeks and the days.

"The new little stranger," some babes are called,
    But that's not what you're going to be;
With double my virtues and half of my faults,
    You can't be a stranger to me.

Your mother is straight as a sapling plant,
    The cleanest and best of her clan—
You're bone of her bone and flesh of her flesh,
    And, by heaven, we'll make you a man.

Soon I shall take you in two strong arms—
    You that shall howl for joy—
With a simple, passionate, wonderful pride
    Because you are just my boy.

And you shall lie in your mother's arms
    And croon at your mother's breast,
And I shall thank God I am there to shield
    The two that I love the best.

A wonderful thing is a breaking wave
    And sweet is the scent of spring,
But the silent voice of an unborn babe
    Is God's most beautiful thing.

We're listening now to that silent voice
    And waiting, your mother and I —
Waiting to welcome the fruit of our love
    When you come to us by and by.

We're hungry to show you a wonderful world
    With wonderful things to be done;
We're aching to give you the best of us both,
    And we're lonely for you — my son.

—CAPTAIN CYRIL MORTON THORNE

AWAITING BABY'S ARRIVAL   33

Baby's Here!

BABY'S HERE
. . . CONGRATULATIONS

Who would have thought
Such tiny hands
So tightly furled
Could hold my heart . . .
My brightest dreams . . .
My very world.
— MONA K. GULDSWOG

BOND

I am enchanted by this blessed mystery—
why you, of all possible infants,
and I, of all possible mothers,
meet here and now to stare with wonder
deeply into one another's eyes.

—MAUREEN TOLMAN FLANNERY

Upon Her Soothing Breast

Upon her soothing breast
She lulled her little child;
A winter sunset in the west,
A dreary glory smiled.

— Emily Brontë

My Baby Has No Name Yet

My baby has no name yet;
like a new-born chick or a puppy,
my baby is not named yet.

What numberless texts I examined
at dawn and night and evening over again!
But not one character did I find
which is as lovely as the child.

Starry field of the sky
or heap of pearls in the depth.
Where can the name be found, how can I?

My baby has no name yet;
like an unnamed bluebird or white flowers
from the farthest land for the first,
I have no name for this baby of ours.

— KIM NAM JO
   TRANSLATED BY KO WAN

INFANT JOY

"I have no name;
I am but two days old."
What shall I call thee?
"I happy am,
Joy is my name."
Sweet joy befall thee!

Pretty joy!
Sweet joy, but two days old.
Sweet joy I call thee;
Thou dost smile,
I sing the while;
Sweet joy befall thee!

—WILLIAM BLAKE

WHERE DID YOU COME FROM?

Where did you come from, Baby dear?
Out of the everywhere into here.

Where did you get your eyes so blue?
Out of the sky as I came through.

What makes the light in them sparkle and spin?
Some of the starry spikes left in.

Where did you get that little tear?
I found it waiting when I got here.

What makes your forehead so smooth and high?
A soft hand stroked it as I went by.

What makes your cheek like a warm white rose?
I saw something better than anyone knows.

Whence that three-corner'd smile of bliss?
Three angels gave me at once a kiss.

Where did you get this pearly ear?
God spoke, and it came out to hear.

Where did you get those arms and hands?
Love made itself into hooks and bands.

Feet, whence did you come, you darling things?
From the same box as the cherubs' wings.

How did they all come just to be you?
God thought of me, and so I grew.

But how did you come to us, you dear?
God thought of you, and so I am here.

— GEORGE MACDONALD

ONLY

Something to live for came to the place,
Something to die for maybe,
Something to give even sorrow a grace,
And yet it was only a baby!

Cooing and laughter and gurgles and cries,
Dimples for tenderest kisses,
Chaos of hopes and of raptures and sighs,
Chaos of fears and of blisses.

Last year, like all years, the rose and the thorn;
This year a wilderness maybe;
But heaven stooped under the roof on the morn
That it brought them only a baby!
— HARRIET PRESCOTT SPOFFORD

The Picture

The painter has with his brush
Transferred the landscape to the canvas
With such fidelity that the trees and grasses
Seem almost real.
He has made even the face
Of a maiden seem instinct with life;
But there is one picture so beautiful
That no painter has ever been able
Perfectly to reproduce it,
And that is the picture of the mother
Holding in her arms her babe.

—William Jennings Bryan

MOTHER'S GARDEN

A fresh little bud in my garden,
With petals close folded from view,
Brightly nods me a cheery "Good morning"
Through the drops of a fresh bath of dew.

I must patiently wait its unfolding,
Though I long its full beauty to see;
Leave soft breezes and warm, tender sunshine
To perform the sweet office for me.

I may shield my fair baby blossom;
With trellis its weakness uphold;
With nourishment wisely sustain it
And cherish its pure heart of gold.

Then in good time, which is God's time,
Developed by sunshine and shower,
Some morning I'll find in the garden
Where my bud was, a beautiful flower.

—AUTHOR UNKNOWN

The Chair by the Window

Your rhythmic nursing slows. I feel
your smile before I see it: nipple pinched
in corner of mouth, your brimming, short,
tuck-cornered smile. I shake my head, my *no* vibrates
to you through ribs and arms. Your tapered ears
quiver, work faintly and still pinker, my
nipple spins right out and we
are two who sit and smile into each other's eyes.

Again, you frowning farmer, me your cow:
you flap one steadying palm against my breast,
thump down the other, chuckle, snort, and then
you're suddenly under, mouth moving steadily, eyes
drifting past mine abstracted, your familiar
blue remote and window-paned with light.

—ANNE WINTERS

BABY'S HERE!

ON CHILDREN

You may give them your love
    But not your thoughts,
For they have their own thoughts.
You may house their bodies
    But not their souls,
For their souls dwell
    In the house of tomorrow,
    Which you may not visit,
    Not even in your dreams.
You may strive to be like them
    But seek not to make them like you,
For life goes not backward
    Nor tarries with yesterday.
You are the bows from which your children
    As living arrows are sent forth.

—KAHLIL GIBRAN

Night Light

Only your plastic night light dusts its pink
on the backs and undersides of things; your mother,
head resting on the nightside of one arm,
floats a hand above your cradle

POEMS FOR A NEW MOTHER

to feel the humid tendril of your breathing.
Outside, the night rocks, murmurs . . . Crouched
in this eggshell light, I feel my heart
slowing, opened to your tiny flame
as if your blue irises mirrored me,
as if your smile breathed and warmed
and curled in your face which is only asleep.
There is space between me, I know,
and you. I hang above you like a planet—
you're a planet, too. One planet loves the other.
—ANNE WINTERS

AS BABY
GROWS

A Wish for My Children

On this doorstep I stand
year after year
and watch you leaving

and think: May you not
skin your knees. May you
not catch your fingers
in car doors. May
your hearts not break.

May tide and weather
wait for your coming

and may you grow strong
to break
all webs of my weaving.

— Evangeline Paterson

ENDEARING CHARMS

Believe me, if all those endearing young charms,
Which I gaze on so fondly today,
Were to change by tomorrow and fleet in my arms
Like fairy gifts fading away,
Thou wouldst still be adored, as this moment thou art.
Let thy loveliness fade as it will
And around the dear ruin each wish of my heart
Would entwine itself verdantly still.

It is not while beauty and youth are thine own
And thy cheeks unprofaned by a tear

That the fervor and faith of a soul may be known
To which time will but make thee more dear!
No, the heart that has truly loved never forgets,
But as truly as loves on to the close,
As the sunflower turns on her god
    when he sets
The same look which she turned
    when he rose.

—THOMAS MOORE

COLLAGE: MOTHER, DAUGHTER, CHILD, AND BOOK

She sits in her grandmother's
rocker, nursing her child.
Her bare feet creak the pair
back and forth on splintered

   legs. Her unsunned breast
    glows in the afternoon
      light like a crescent moon,
       her nipple is a milky peak

that the child, full of itself,
lets go; he sleeps now
in a crater of her flesh.
The mother is not asleep,

she holds a book. Her arms
embrace the child like planets
circling an earth; her head
thrusts forward as if to ward off

guilt, and she reads. I know
from the way the book quivers
in her hands, and the green eyes
narrow like a river racing

underground, that she is far
away, at sea; she is pumping
herself up with oysters, she is
breeding pearls in her pap.

Soon she will feed it
to the child, but in these few
moments while her son sleeps,
she thinks only of her book,

the way a parched woman gulps
from a cup with both hands
and the milk spills,
unnoticed, on the child's cheek.
—NANCY MEANS WRIGHT

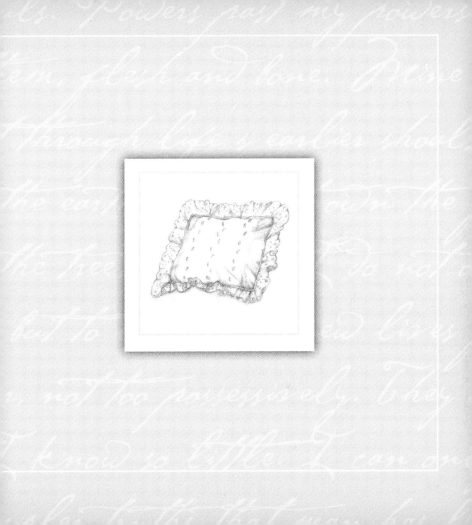

from DUET FOR ONE VOICE

We escape from our mothers
again and again, young
Houdinis playing the usual matinees.
First comes escape down
the birth canal, our newly carved faces
leading the way like figureheads
on ancient slave ships,
our small hands rowing for life.

Later escape into silence, escape
behind slammed doors,
the flight into marriage.

I thought I was finally old enough
to sit with you, sharing a book.
But when I look up from the page, you
have escaped from me.

—LINDA PASTAN

THERE ARE TIMES IN LIFE WHEN ONE DOES THE RIGHT THING

the thing one will not regret,
when the child wakes crying "mama," late
as you are about to close your book and sleep
and she will not be comforted back to her crib,
she points you out of her room, into yours,
you tell her, "I was just reading here in bed,"
she says, "read a book," you explain it's not a
    children's book
but you sit with her anyway, she lays her head
    on your breast,

one-handed, you hold your small book, silently read,
resting it on the bed to turn pages
and she, thumb in mouth, closes her eyes, drifts,
not asleep—when you look down at her, her lids open,
and once you try to carry her back
but she cries, so you return to your bed again and book,
and the way a warmer air will replace a cooler
    with a slight
shift of wind, or swimming, entering a mild current, you
enter this pleasure, the quiet book, your daughter
    in your lap,

an articulate person now, able to converse, yet still
her cry is for you, her comfort in you,
it is your breast she lays her head upon,
you are lovers, asking nothing but this bodily presence.
She hovers between sleep, you read your book,
you give yourself this hour, sweet and quiet
    beyond flowers
beyond lilies of the valley and lilacs even, the smell of
    her breath,
the warm damp between her head and your breast.

Past midnight
she blinks her eyes, wiggles toward a familiar position,
utters one word, "sleeping." You carry her swiftly
　　into her crib,
cover her, close the door halfway, and it is this sense
　　of rightness,
that something has been healed, something
you will never know, will never have to know.

— ELLEN BASS

JOURNEY

Your small hand still clings tightly to my own
Along dark halls to hush your little fears;
Yet you will cross this darkened hall alone,
Unfearing, in the span of a few years.
You come to me still with your woe and joy
(My heart is humbled by your trusting eyes),
And I am glad you're still a little boy
Who thinks that I am kind and strong and wise.

And when your small hand clings to mine no more,
May you have found some worthy work to do.
And may your eager heart behold a score
Of dreams; may love and courage see you through
Upon the journey you have just begun.
My heart enfolds this prayer for you, my son.

—MARGARET H. HASBARGEN

My Children

My children are not mine. I do not own
   Their small, dear bodies, least of all, their souls.
Powers past my powers have built them, flesh and bone.
   Mine but to pilot through life's earlier shoals.

I am the earth; I do not own the flower.
   I am the tree; the fruit I do not own.
Mine but to love these new lives for the hour,
   Not too possessively. They are Time's loan.

I know so little. I can only teach

  The simpler truths that man has learned to trust;
Help them to gracious ways of thought and speech,

  Then let them go their way; for go they must.
— MARJORIE KINNAN RAWLINGS

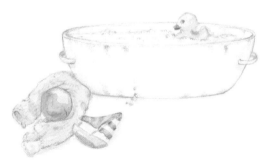

LULLABIES
FOR BABY

Lullaby, Oh, Lullaby

Lullaby, oh, lullaby!
Flowers are closed and lambs are sleeping;
Lullaby, oh, lullaby!
Stars are up, the moon is peeping;
Lullaby, oh, lullaby!
While the birds are silence keeping,
Lullaby, oh, lullaby!
Sleep, my baby, fall a-sleeping,
Lullaby, oh, lullaby!

—Christina Rossetti

GOOD NIGHT

Little baby, lay your head
Upon your pretty cradle bed
And shut your eye-peeps now that day
And all the light have gone away.

Yes, my sweet darling, well I know
How the bitter wind doth blow;
And the winter's snow and rain
Patter on the windowpane.

Little baby, lay your head
Upon your pretty cradle bed
And shut your eye-peeps now that day
And all the light have gone away.

For the window shuts so fast
Till the stormy night is past,
And the curtains warm are spread
Round about your cradle bed.

Little baby, lay your head
Upon your pretty cradle bed
And shut your eye-peeps now that day
And all the light have gone away.

— JANE TAYLOR

Mother's Song

My heart is like a fountain true
That flows and flows with love to you.
As chirps the lark unto the tree,
So chirps my pretty babe to me.

And it's oh, sweet, sweet;
And it's oh, sweet, sweet;
And it's oh, sweet, sweet;
My baby's lullaby.

—English Lullaby

The Road to Slumber Land

What is the road to Slumber Land?
Tell me, when does the baby go?
The road is so straight through Mother's arms,
And the sun is sinking low.

Poems for a New Mother

This is the way, through Mother's arms,
All little babies go.
This is the road to Slumber Land
When the sun is sinking low.

Soft little gown so clean and white
And a face washed so sweet and fair —
A mother with love is brushing out
All the tangles in baby's hair.

This is the way, through Mother's arms,
All little babies go.
This is the road to Slumber Land
When the sun is sinking low.

—MARY D. BRINE

SWEET AND LOW

Sweet and low, sweet and low,
Wind of the western sea does blow.
Sweet and low, sweet and low,
Wind of the western sea does blow.

Over the rolling waters go,
Come from the dropping moon, and blow,
Blow him again to me while my little one,
While my pretty one sleeps tonight.

Sweet and low, sweet and low,
Wind of the western sea does blow.
Sweet and low, sweet and low,
Wind of the western sea does blow.

Sleep and rest, sleep and rest,
Rest on your loving mother's breast.
Sleep and rest, sleep and rest,
Rest on your loving mother's breast.

Father will come to his babe in the nest
Like silver sails out of the west;
Under the silver moon, sleep, my little one,
Sleep, my little one, sleep tonight.

Sleep and rest, sleep and rest,
Rest on your loving mother's breast.
Sleep and rest, sleep and rest,
    Rest on your loving mother's breast.

—ALFRED, LORD TENNYSON

TITLE INDEX

AUTHOR INDEX

POEMS FOR A NEW MOTHER

FIRST LINE INDEX

On this doorstep I stand, 57
Only your plastic night light dusts its pink, 54
She sits in her grandmother's, 60
Something to live for came to the place, 44
Suddenly, you are. In an instant, 22
Sweet and low, sweet and low, 82
The earth needs only nature, 24
The love of a mother is never exhausted, 12
The painter has with his brush, 47
The thing one will not regret, 66
Upon her soothing breast, 37
We escape from our mothers, 64
What is the road to Slumber Land, 80
When God thought of mother, 7
Where did you come from, Baby dear, 42
Who fed me from her gentle breast, 18
Who would have thought, 35
Womanliness means only motherhood, 9
You may give them your love, 52
Your rhythmic nursing slows. I feel, 50
Your small hand still clings tightly to my own, 70